ABRACADABRA

Poetry

Olivia Ngozi Osuoha

Mwanaka Media and Publishing Pvt Ltd,
Chitungwiza, Zimbabwe
*
Creativity, Wisdom, and Beauty

Publisher: *Mmap*
Mwanaka Media and Publishing Pvt Ltd
24 Svosve Road, Zengeza 1
Chitungwiza, Zimbabwe
mwanaka@yahoo.com
mwanaka13@gmail.com
https://www.mmapublishing.org
www.africanbookscollective.com/publishers/mwanaka-media-and-publishing
https://facebook.com/MwanakaMediaAndPublishing/

Distributed in and outside N. America by African Books Collective
orders@africanbookscollective.com
www.africanbookscollective.com

ISBN: 978-1-77933-850-1
EAN: 9781779338501

© Olivia Ngozi Osuoha 2024

All rights reserved.
No part of this book may be reproduced or transmitted in any form or by any means, mechanical or electronic, including photocopying and recording, or be stored in any information storage or retrieval system, without written permission from the publisher

DISCLAIMER
All views expressed in this publication are those of the author and do not necessarily reflect the views of *Mmap*.

Table of contents

Introduction
This Land
The Mystery of Ignorance
Pepper Red
Hymn
Red Alert
Our Parents didn't Fail
They Said it didn't happen
Don't Renew my Hope
They have Come again
Asking for a Friend
Be your Flamingo
Dear Dollar
Wolves in Sheep's Clothing
Lord we Pray
To whom it may Concern
I Want to Visit the Chantham House
Dear Qatar
Parallel People
Eight Days to Election Nigeria to Decide
Freedom is Coming Tomorrow
Buffalo Soldier
On the Borderline
Abracadabra
Eluu Pee
The Coconut Head has Changed the Narrative
Dear Charles Solido
My Two Billion Dollars
Twilight of Honour
Dear Kingley Moghalu

Happy Biryhday to the Village Girl
The Town Crier
The State and its Gate
Shame to God
Ladies, Model yourselves
Burnt Orange
I am Afraid
All the Eyes on the Judiciary
Hearty Bongo Noise
 Chief Cargo
Time will Tell
Dear Single Lady
Mmap New African Poets Series

Introduction

F. Scot Fitzgerald rightly said "writers aren't exactly people ...they are a whole bunch of people trying to be one person" that is what this writer is buttressing in her book "ABRACADABRA"

She succeeded in imbedding mysteries under her lines, tones, words and thoughts. As she normally refers to herself as "The Village Girl", one may be deceived by the actual meaning of this book whether read or unread.

Each verse, and each poem or poetic prose has diverse meanings and real thoughts away from the context and what the eyes can see. She battled horrors and evils going on in both the true and imaginative worlds, hence her call-out against the pain, like everything is going abracadabra, like a tale, a funny fairy tale.

Hence, a thorough reading, meditation and interpretation is required to digest this piece of work. It is general and universal, not truly portraying the face value of the written words and chosen titles. Think deep, ponder anew, dig further. And see that this work is beyond the ordinary, beyond the imaginative and around the weirdest.

Sincerely, we do hope that you enjoy, learn, grow and change after reading the book, ABRACADABRA. If we have a better world, we all would benefit from it, likewise if we have an evil and ugly world.

Therefore, one can easily see that change is possible if we believe and if we work towards it. We should not fail to know and note that, change of a truth, begins with us, each of us, just you and I.

THIS LAND

This land, where certificates are sold on shopping malls.

This land, where power is might, might is power and might is right.

This land, where only leaders exist.

This land, where lamentations are the masses' anthem.

This land, where the air is extremely contaminated.

This land, where natural resources look like curses.

This land, where poverty and hardship rule as lord.

This land, where siblings will never agree.

This land, where everyone is a suspect.

This land, where only the poor and the innocent go to jail.

This land, where money is the only language.

This land, where deceit and betrayal are the offsprings.

This land, where the truth remains in the grave.

This land, where no word is true.

This land, whose unborn generations are already given away.

This land, that is swampy and flooded with blood.

This land, where natural disaster is equivalent to the horrors.

This land, where stealing is a credit.

This land, where professionalism is the opposite.

This land, where killing gives pleasure.

DO YOU PRAY FOR THIS LAND?

THE MYSTERY OF IGNORANCE

If you see my teacher, tell him he didn't waste his time.

Please tell him that though the world has messed with his toils, tell him that I will never forget him, nor his tools.

Tell my teacher though, the society has belittled him and crushed him, please tell him that he is very precious in my heart and mind.

Tell my teacher that my soul longs to reward him, wherever he is. God, help me.

Don't forget to tell my teacher that I was never stubborn nor stupid, I was only being a child.

Please help tell my teacher that he was never wicked, I only misinterpreted and misunderstood him.

Tell my alma maters, that they can never rot, as long as I live. I will find their blocks and bricks and lay them back perfectly someday.

Tell my chapels, that they still lift my soul till tomorrow. Let the hymns and prayers continue.

Please help me thank my teacher, bless them on my behalf. Reach out to them. How and what could I have been without them?

I promise I will never let you down, be you my teacher or my alma mater.

Your memory is golden and diamond. Thank you for having me. And most importantly, for raising me!

PEPPER RED

As I articulate, I realize I am not from the north.
Hence as I lag behind, the thief goes on to rotten the already bad situation.

My heart is not dark, but my skin is darkening like I am from the north.
The sun and water here don't look harsh, but daily I grow dark.
Please help me, I can't articulate.

I wear pepper red, is the pepper entering your eyes? It's not resilience. It's not creativity. It's wickedness!

I come from the East, and that's where the sun rises! The sun is obedient, hence it will always rise, come what may.

Bags and barrels of oil in thousands don't traverse, they don't build bridges if the east has been bombed after and since independence.

This red is pepper, it is peppering me at parallel lines, are forcing confluence and interceptions without correspondence and alternates.

If a northern Cameroonian hemisphere with so high an altitude, linking attitude with latitude and longitude, hence causing the equator to suffer Capricorn of Cancer, then the earth will either be as hot as the Mars or as cold as the Pluto.

A bigot can beget maggot, and a maggot-infested farmer will have his farm destroyed.

If you couldn't treat my teacher-parents well, you will assassinate my dad in my presence if he was a brigadier, and then bring me wreath and plaque.

See, Octobus will never forget lekki. And October will be immotalized. Toll it or not. The end is the beginning. The youths are not lazy, they don't japa for treatment and rest, rather for greener pasture.

Your pan can only fry anger, revenge, pride and arrogance. Pan-not, pan-tweet, pan-bat, pounding same ticket.

My job is done. Sit down on my seat. Onye kwuru that thing??

HYMN

Dear God, dear Lord, watch over me,
In this strangest of lands
My eyes, my mind can't see the realms
Fighting to have my life!

With thee, my life safe, sound and sane
Bubbling in might and health,
The foe waiting in vain and pain
Lurking, losing the war!

Arise my helper, strong and firm
Lift my soul from the dust,
I know nothing, I see nothing
Dear Lord, in thee assured.

I dare not trust my feeble sense
Nor run with my poor legs,
My strength cannot fathom the fight
My might will fail again.

Today, I hope I do not rot
The future thou know all,
The past has all the bleeding part
The all, the all thou know.

Hear me Lord from thy throne on high
Rescue thy little pet,
Heal me, heal us, heal them, heal all
The world belongs to thee.

Amen.

*(Ready to shower, before this hymn was inspired, I had no option than to drop it
Tune: how sweet the name of Jesus sounds)*

RED ALERT

On top of my head is a structure, I am not a saboteur.
I am not a unifier cooking corn to feed armies, and to line up beggars beyond territories.

Alerts rotten, as monkeys swallow vaults. Bad eggs smell as snakes crawl in and outside rocks, rocks of capitals.

Leaders retreat and surrender as rodents present prudent embezzlement.

Unifier equals fire. Firing secretariats and banks.

Red alert! Cattle have finished cassava farms. Maize has become a sacrilege. Farmers farm famine and females frame felony.

Voting coats, coats of many colours. Colours that mar rainbows. Carding thunders, thunders that strike heavens.

Age to age, back to back, they wander, afar off. Looting, looting treasures. Driving me crazy and lazy.

Utensils of partisanship. Partisans of crude wickedness, wickedness of total cruise. Cruising in chains, chains of enslaved lands.

Abattoirs, maiming life. Planting deaths.

On this little head, lies pain. Sorrow that glitter back and forth. Navigating climes, climes of poisonous crimes. Criminal gods, demonic lords. They are thirsty, thirsty of blood. Their own blood.

Hospitals kill, schools brainwash, religions dehumanize. A land of fairly tales, tales of inhumanity.

Contracts are contacted, workers are worked off, labours are lured in. Hail this hell, heavens heavily hiss.

Tear up, tear down. Wear out, wear off. Shout, blow the trumpet. Ring the alarm, set the time. It's only for the time-bomb.

Overflow of hunger, abuse of blood, negligence of deities, incompetence of spirits, in the end if you can manage to patch your throat.

Red head, red hat, red heart, red eyes, red soul, red count, red control, the land is red, dangerously bleeding.

I am not a saboteur. I am a structure. I am obeying my passion. But how did we turn red, and why did we turn this land, red- a land flowing with milk and honey?

Tell the saboteur that the night is here, and tomorrow is no longer far. That tomorrow, is the day of reckoning.

Banners, t-shirts, wrappers, rice, salt, umbrellas, monies and empty promises filled with threats will not take any one to paradise.

It's a red alert, the pain is spilling over. Let this land heal.

OUR PARENTS DIDN'T FAIL

My parents fell into one generation. I will never believe their generation failed, never!!!

Dad fought the Biafran war, mum witnessed the war. I listen to them tell stories of the war.

Mum talks like a witness, Dad talks like a partaker, a soldier, that's why my sixth book *WHISPERS OF THE BIAFRAN SKELETON* was dedicated to him.

The climax is that he was so brave that he sneaked out of the house from my hometown around 2am, trekked to Okigwe and got enlisted in the Biafran Army. What more could be so patriotic and historical??

Both of them were/are teachers. They groomed and disciplined thousands throughout their 70 years of service, (35 + 35).

It was Nigeria that failed my parents. They put in their best, integrity, honesty, strength, energy despite government's insincerity, insensitivity, carelessness and wickedness.

The government turned teachers and teaching in Nigeria into a nightmare. That's why when people ask me to go into teaching, they don't understand or know my anger, bitterness, and disappointment.

Dad retired in 2006 as a principal, but till date, he hasn't gotten his gratuity. Mum, a few years later, hasn't gotten hers too.

In fact, their pensions are in the hand of God.

They were lucky enough to be blessed with good health, strength, energy, children, and grace. Some of their fellows are still training their children in primary, secondary, tertiary institutions. Some were more fortunate and blessed though. Many are sick, bedridden, hopeless, and helpless. Many have died in queues waiting for their pensions, capturing, documentation,....

A governor once compelled them to sign off their arrears, that they have been paid. Being a Nigerian is punishment. Only God can work out some miracles.

The Nigerian government is demonic, ungodly and evil. Whatever is political here is ungodly.

But our leaders have paradises abroad.

Imagine if Osibanjo or Buhari had a daughter like me, world presidents would be launching their books.

Nigeria is Cruel! I am a witness!

THEY SAID IT DIDN'T HAPPEN

Today, two years back Nigeria struck,
Nigeria struck Nigeria, in the land of Nigeria against Nigerians.
It didn't happen anyway.

People agitating for good governance got fired.
They had their intestines wired,
And their hands holding national flags cut off.
Don't mind me, it never happened.

Thugs were let loose, upon innocent youths.
Terror was unleashed on the leaders of tomorrow, maiming some, wounding some, killing some.
Some swam to their death, near lekki, around lekki, beside lekki, in Lagos.
Be happy, relax, it's a crap. Fabricated!
Power and might said nothing like that ever happened.

The national anthem was on, yet the National Guard released bullets, bullets on peaceful protesters. This day in history! Not true, though.

Uniforms denied, after flexing power, and flying guns.
They camouflaged and masked the ugly incident.
They sabotaged the green blood they spilled, staining the colours of their coat of arm.
Louder, they shout and still prove that it didn't happen.

On this day in history, gave birth to Sagent Fash. Looking and searching for cam, camera and cctv. Days after the incident, cleaning and rains. Nigeria proved that lekki massacre never occurred

States took turns in anger, uncovering stores of pallatives. Palliatives for hungry Nigerians. Fellow Nigerians stored and piled them up, starving those who sent them to serve them. Yet, it didn't happen.

Sorosoke! Speak up, it didn't happen.
End Sars, end police brutality, end wickedness, it happened in the land of dreams.

Families lost loved ones, victims spoke out, juries were set. Representatives were sent. Fines and cost were awarded. Evidences came out, yet these people disbelieved and disproved lekki massacre. How then did it happen?

Have you seen our national flag lately? Since the twentieth of October, two years back, at the peak of covid?
It didn't happen!
The Facebook live, the whole world following and watching were blind. They saw nothing, they said nothing. Nothing happened. Lekki massacre was a movie, a fairy tale.

It was a lie, yet they were teargassed, even today.
They were bullied, arrested, intimidated, big lie.
EndSars was a national ceremony. Honouring national integrity.

They disbanded SARS, but it was a lie. They turned to SWAT, still a lie. Because there was no victim.

People cooked, contributed, gifted, donated, made unbelievable sacrifices, yet Nigeria said it didn't happen, with proofs.

Sorosoke! The wrong generation. Coconut head. Pressing phone generation. Analog desperately fighting to wipe away digital age. I am sorry, nothing happened. I am kidding you.

Strong yoke, shaken together, pressed down, running over, on the neck of this generation. Because they sorosoke-ed. Lekki, is still crying. I can hear her, weeping again today in remembrance.

Gunshots, chaos, bloods, stains, lekki was very peaceful. That tollgate never saw blood. Live bullets were picked there, then and later, yet it was a lie.

Local and foreign reporters were there, saved by grace, yet the massacre was a groove.

Viral live videos and photos were tagged fake news, because their loved ones were abroad, safe and sound. So nobody died at lekki tollgate.

The switch that switched on the Armageddon, was whisked away for safety. Others were placed on surveillance. Fairy tale!

How else can a government mean meanness?

If you sorosoke, they lekk-tollgate your coconut head, and call it fake news. They own the media. They own the uniforms. They own the forces, they are the might and mighty!

If the CCTV has to be repaired on this day in history, and the lights went off on this day in history, then the uniforms arrived shooting peaceful protesters waving the national flag, dressed in national colours, singing the national anthem, then lekki massacre is a fairy tale. It didn't happen, because they said so!

Now, they want to recruit us into the army and serve us agbado, ewa, maize, poisoned holy communion, and climate change even when bandits, terrorists, herdsman, flood and famine have killed both the farmer and consumer.

If the northern pole obeys the sun, the four cardinal points will not be flying to the moon for treatment, because the sun will heal the land.

On this day in history, they said the crystal stars of EndSars never shone up above the sky. That's what they said. They said it didn't happen!

DON'T RENEW MY HOPE

They came in their droves, grooving change. We begged, prayed, pleaded and preached but they called us wailers. Today, it's like no one is weeping, or everyone has joined the wailing team.

They wrapped a messiah in a mannequin or a mannequin in a messiah, and hoisted up, like a waving flag. The flag, pigeons and doves, all have refused to fly.

All pleas fell on deaf ears, and all ears went deaf, because they were blind and lame.

The change that buried hope, and had hope unleash terror. Terror on hopes, hopeful faithful on the land

Unknown gun-ment and known gun-mental syndicates cooking apocalypse, paralysing the change in all hopeless ways.

They changed brooms to giants, yet couldn't sweep and renewed giants to brooms yet refused to sweep. Now, flood is helping them sweep a whole country away. Prepare for hunger and famine.

The dollar was changed, and now they want to renew the hopelessness.

A bag of rice was changed, a bag of cement they changed, egg changed, biscuits changed, beans did, everything changed. Humans drastically changed, now they want the hopelessness renewed. God forbid this hope!

Hoping against hope, wishful thinking. False living. This changeful hope is better not renewed.

Enough of the torture. The slavery is already enough. Embezzlement is overboard. This hope is not renewal. Terms and conditions apply!

Brooms that can't sweep, sweepers that sold brooms, sweeping brooms that messed up everywhere. You had better not renewed this hope!

Crude, petrol, kero, diesel, all swept away. Flood sweeping off the land. Cassava, flour, maize, all gone! Who swept this land? Please don't renew our hope with trouble!

Walk into the gym, and touch your toes.
Ride a bicycle and tour the france,
Wear a suit for a photoshoot,
Read me the constitutional manifesto
This hope of mine you can't renew!

London bridge, Burj Khalifa, the CCTV and the lights that went off, and the shots, who gave the order? Which hope do you want to renew? What about change? Has change finally gone clueless?

Climate change is hazardous, apc-rial change is disastrously, how can one renew hope in the face of hopelessness?

Don't renew my hope if the change you promised me was unchangeful, this hope renewal would be deadly.

My hope is built on nothing less than Jesus blood, this flood of national complex and territorial tussle won't change or renew our hope.

Hopeless change and changeless hope cannot change the hope or hope for a change, therefore let me be.

We will not labour in vain, because power belongs to the people, and that only can bring the actual change that will renew hope, otherwise a bunch of cleaners sweep in vain.

THEY HAVE COME AGAIN

The season is here, and the reason very crystal, power!

The tussle is on, and the battle line has been drawn. Morale and moral will be endangered whether engendered or not.

It's time, they will soon start selling pure water and roast corn by the roadside or near the gutters.

They will soon be visiting schools to wine and dine with pupils, and make sure it's all over the media.

See them, they will soon start buying roasted plantain, fried fish, cooked corn and pears. It's time to be humble like a common Nigerian, whose life doesn't count.

Time to stop their convoys and help accident victims, to show empathy and sympathy, even when their one-way-lane drive caused it or to show us that they don't drive private jets anymore.

They will soon start buying sugarcane, tiger nuts, cherries, and mobile articles in trucks. To show us that they bleed red and breathe air.

Politics; my wayward brother. He will soon open his mouth wide and rain promises like flood. Talking without thinking. Of course, with round of applause. Why won't he be applauded?

Time to locate town halls, village squares, market places, religious shrines, altars of diverse powers. The time has come. It's now!

Watch and pray, my people. The enemy tires not. He's roaming about and roaring, instead of soaring. Be mindful of his devices. These wolves.

They are shameless, they don't get tired of fake promises. They neither sleep nor slumber, provided their trap is set. Set by the river, forest, home and abroad.

You will see them enter motorcycles, keke, taxis and public buses now, because they want to appear Nigerian, local, rural, down to earth and humane.

The point is I can't comprehend the face with which they promise, and the one with which they lie, counter and contradict themselves.

They have finished words; foreign and local. They have finished dramas; action and oral. They have finished chances; games and plays.
I don't know what else they would do.

They are here again, they have come again. I am tired of looking at or listening to them. These people fear nothing, in fact, God himself fears them.

They have come again, all over again they have come. How can I resist them? Because they have cantankerously come to kill, in unism to steal, loot and destroy.

Tell them to prove me wrong. I dare them to fix this country. Is democracy demonic? Is the barber or baba barbaric?

Is it a curse to be Nigerian or a Nigerian? Is the giant of Africa a dwarf? Or he was stunted? Why do the rich also cry?

Things have fallen apart
We are no longer at ease
It is not the arrow of god,
Therefore the gods must be crazy.

ASKING FOR A FRIEND

Unlike 50 Cent, I have some 21 questions to ask. I doubt if I would get answers because I am asking for a friend.

How do ladies wear plastics inside their breasts and still flaunt it to the world, for applause? We get it, though.

How do we ladies in this generation especially, build-in plastics and rubbers in our hips and still go nude for approval and celebration? They are being celebrated anyway.

How do my ladies constantly wear artificial hairs longer than the knees, not mindful of the emergencies and risks therein? Men love it, of course.

How do we ladies wear fans on our eyelids and think we have arrived? Some have gone blind fixing and or removing whether contacts or lashes. We don't learn after all.

Why do we ladies wear half clothes leaving our breasts to the public all the time, is there something about breasts that we are missing as women?

Those of us who feel inferior for not wearing attachments, are there any values these attachments add to our personalities? Just asking for a friend!

Those of us who steal or prostitute for big phones,... after calls, texts, chats, businesses, pictures, tiktok and online noise, which other fame are we going for? My friend is still asking!

These handbags that come from abroad, when will we start carrying human heads in them? Answer!

Those hilly heels, do they help us touch Kilimanjaro or Everest? My friend said I should ask.

Men, how do you feel walking along the street with a sane naked or half-naked lady? You don't need to answer me, I am asking for a friend.

Ladies, how do we feel painting all the colours on our face to look good, when we actually frighten people? My friend said I should ask you.

These long claws that can't change fate, why do we need them? Irritating, dangerously and weird! My friend is asking!

Is anything wrong with nature, even when it's the most beautiful and amazing? Please answer my friend.

What is peer pressure? Why is wrong influence the most gravitational?

You see humans, you wonder where you are and in the midst of what creatures you are. Is beauty all about poster colours and plastic surgery? Just asking for a friend.

Who told you that you must look a definite shape, have a specific height or wear a particular fashion to have a sense of belonging?

When did bleaching become audacious? The audacity of ignorance and stupidity is burying this generation alive. How did we get here?

Whoever taught you that you must have drawings on your body and skin to tell your stories is a false teacher. Avoid him!

Ladies, whoever taught you that getting high and drunk, qualifies you for a slay queen is your enemy. Run as fast as you can!

Dreams are incubated and hatched, they are not smoked, drank, drunk or tattooed to reality. Get it right!

If you think your shape, size, face, breasts, legs, complexion, wig, lashes, handbags, shoes, and the likes are what you need to slay, then you have already been slayed and slew!

Asking for a friend, don't you think it's high time we made amends.... because this generation of ladies makes being a lady unacceptable.

BE YOUR FLAMINGO

If you are from Congo
You may not have a mango,
If you love indigo
You may not have libido,
If you play with dildo
It may not make you a virgo,
So be your flamingo
Because the world is not rooting for you!

No matter the cargo
It could miss its way to Togo,
If you hail from Trinidad and Tobago
It does not guarantee your ludo,
So lift the embargo
If you hate to be a bingo,
Be your own flamingo
If you want the world to root for you.

The government will trim your wings
And even hide your rings,
They will give you some stings
And distort all your songs,
Just be a flamingo
Then the world will root for you!

You might win some bronze
Or the one they froze,

You could acquire some silver
And become a diva,
You might also get some gold
And then go so bold,
Only then they will root for you.

Nobody is rooting for you
Root, route and enroute yourself
Be your flamingo!

Wade the sea, your legs are long, don't underestimate them
Fly the sky, your wings are light, don't belittle them,
Your neck can bear the yoke, it's long and flexible
The world isn't looking out for you!

You, yourself and you alone,
You are the bone
Build up your cone,
You are the crane
Lift up your plane,
Run, yours alone is the lane.

Be your flamingo, lift the embargo
So that you don't forgo your cargo.

DEAR DOLLAR

Deeds of dubious men deal directly and indirectly, they dry and dirty densities.

Deaf and dumb deities dignify them and make them demigods.

Dangers degenerate to deaths and ditches, because volcanoes can't turn avacados.

Dragons disintegrate to dooms and draculas decimate doves, because duties are either abandoned or stoned.

Dogs make dullards out of collars and collars make pillars out of dollars.

Mass dogmas stigmatize the traumatized kobo and the energized dollar dramatize the sabotaged Naira.

Dear dollar, this doll is neither for sex nor self-aggrandizement. The point is that I have a coat, whether or not from a box of rags, rags of many colours.

When polarization has taken place, sensitization and familiarization may not be needful, because forces of pull will either harmonize them in unity or disunity.

Dear domiciliary, digging therefore a rugged dungeon can only land you in dreaded dens.

The dotted spot can get the whole plot rotten if the plotted graph is totally forgotten, hence the masquerade needs to tread with caution because there's a barricade in the parade.

Decades of decadence delay development, dilute peace and neutralize deliberation as dialogues diffuse.

Dear dollar, I am not a dullard, Lugard must have lied to you. Forget the floral aspect.

WOLVES IN SHEEP'S CLOTHING

Some people bear local names, but not actually their tribal names. They pretend to be from specific tribes, but they spit fire. These people are green snakes on green grasses. Beware!

I have come across people here who bear Igbo names, both as first and second names, but they aren't Igbos, they can't, they won't, and they never should, but they talk and say things that Esau who sold his birthright can't dare. This is just to make you hate Igbos. Except you can decipher, you wouldn't believe or know they aren't Igbos.

When I read a write up from an "Igbo" I know, I am likely to know. I hope you understand what I mean.

The aims of these folks and their likes, are to incite, ignite, instigate, stimulate, force and cause you to hate/fight/kill the other.

It is likely to be the same with other tribes too. I believe there are people from other tribes who do the same. Please always sieve what you read. People bear strange local names just to blackmail, scandalize, slander, betray, and harm other tribes.

You can't take away the Igbo blood and Igbo breast milk from any Igbo. Our Igboness is raw, undiluted and unflinching. Hence, strangers who bear our names act, speak, and behave un-Igboly. Unfortunately these fools always have large followers, fans, listeners, and gullible folks. Many a time, they are spies, undercovers, paid agents and sycophants.

Wolves in sheep's clothing, they are devourers!

LORD WE PRAY

Lord, we pray for our families. May you watch over us anywhere and always, from your throne.

Save us from evil friends and horrible relatives who want to set us up, to unleash jungle justice on us. Lord, rise against them.

Speak for us, speak on our behalves, speak to us, speak through us, speak with us and keep speaking. Silence every evil tongue.

Save the innocent, repay the wicked. Justify the just. And glorify your name.

Lord, we are not Jesus, so no Judas shall betray us. We are not John, no Herold shall behead us. Even if we are Joseph, no brothers shall sell us. Though we are Daniel, no Lion shall tamper with us. Even if they pronounce us the prostitute, your mercy shall fault the stoners.

Lord, no weapon formed against us shall prosper. No gang shall intentionally accuse us innocently. Though, they gather...they shall scatter.
Please always grant us escape routes in your mercy. Amen.

THANK YOU LORD.

TO WHOM IT MAY CONCERN (ii)

Politics is a web so interwoven, sandwiched, complicated and complex that campaigns have became written scripts for candidates to perform.

Electoral promises are now illusions and infatuations aimed at fooling the people. They are entertaining languages fashioned to scratch itching ears, hence one must prepare for the worst if one ever clings to any.
The womb of politics is abundantly deceitful and betraying.

Trump won. Hillary won too. Stories abound, beautiful and ugly...those, a political novice like me cannot prove. They have their fame and their name too.
Two things do I pray, one that Trump becomes the best. Two that he never turns the worst because if we must work by day, nature requires that we rest by night.

The least surprise would be speeches defending, supporting, refuting, denying, explaining, and or countering any or all of the campaign hymns, litanies, psalms and chants.

Going by the sound of the bitter kola, it should be sweeter than the honey but when you take a seat, you realise the fierceness of the scorpions biting your buttocks and how befittingly fair your face must remain.
More so, in the land where everyone is a reptile, you either lie down wisely or be forcefully made a reptile. Leadership supersedes winning an election.

If campaign promises were tickets to heaven, no Nigerian dead, alive and or unborn would still be here on earth.

For the historic Obama, I still see a traditional Obama parallel to "some actions".
I pray Mr Black does not quit the White House for a century.

For the prophets who prophesied otherwise, there are times God conceals information or intentionally fools His prophet for whatever reasons best known to Him....one of those moments I presume. Not all prophets understand fellow prophets, not always do they understand God either.

Though he prays the rosary, I fear him; a political Jesus. If a people should be excitedly overwhelmed with expectations from politics within and abroad...honestly IT SHOULD NOT BE NIGERIANS.....shame on me if they deceive me one hundred times.

I WANT TO VISIT THE CHATHAM HOUSE

I am set, off for the Chatham House, look behind me.

I want to chatter like a chatter box, see a Chatter House behind me.

I know nothing to answer, so please don't assign me any question.

I am not a presidential candidate, I am not articulated, I am not a bat, I am only labouring, because a labourer deserves his wages, hence he cannot labour in vain.

Look, see, this Chatham House is royal, institutional, and futuristic, it is neither archaic nor outdated.

The blue barber cannot afford a blue board, hence the blue print is a blurred copy.

I want to visit the Chatham House, hear me dear England. This Nigeria is taking me for a joke.

Do not interview me, I am not coming for a debate. If imperfect was a person, that's me, far from the best, as heaven is far from the earth.

Chatham, this chat is not a pie chart. My heart pants, because these ants rant as my wants taunt my soul.

Oh the housing Chatham, do me no harm, I am a charm, a balm in Gilead. I have come to heal and be healed.

This wound lives here, here in my home. It echoes loud and reverberates aloud. The crowd turns it on, and on.

I am coming to the Chatham House. Mr Speaker, answer for me. Hell will fry, let the corns test the ants...the theft is a receiver, and the receiver is a theft.

There will be eggs for pupils' school fees, that's the issue-based campaign.

Broom, boom, bum, brim, brush brush broom, boo boo. The bee is still singing and stinging.

This Chattering House behind me is the one chattering like a chatter box, wagging my tail like a fairy tale. I am speechless, but then, dear Chatham House, I want to visit you.

DEAR QATAR

If you didn't see our eagles, it doesn't mean they can't fly,
Look at the originals, so aboriginal.

The eagles are soaring, flying to remain super.

They have produced flamingos, falconets, and falcons. Now, they can't cater for Qatar.

A copy of the original, no photocopy, no duplicate, no replicate.

They will not green the eagles, fly the eagles or super the eagles in vain.

Even when they lose, we still celebrate them because their spirits, hearts, bodies and souls played.

If you scored them first, you had just bought and brought trouble upon yourself and your nation. Yes, they were that real.

Their supporters club was the best. They would sing forever. Nothing stops them. Their trumpet was from heaven. Angels enjoyed them, even God.

See this group, this squad, they are like the military, football soldiers. They fought, defended, won, lost, bombed and conquered.

Dear Qatar, if you don't see this troupe, and these troops, the world cup is incomplete. But go on anyway.

This squad will never let you down. The excitement was second to none. This squad bound Nigeria. We never knew.

A formidable force, indomitable, black stars, elephants, soaring squad of Nigeria; the eagles!

Time and tide quieten, name and fame fade, but these ones, this squad is an everlasting best. A national honour, a continental pride.

I don't know how life is programmed, when, where and who. Hence, life has not treated some fairly.

To those who have gone to be with their Maker, keep resting in perfect peace.
To you, who have retired, may age and ageing be on your side.
To those whom we have abandoned, may God remember you.
To those whom we frustrated, may talent be kind to you once more, and also in the world to come.

Nigeria, a land of heavenly stars, a place of divine bodies, yet tribes and tongues divide and rule. Yet, religion and politics shatter and scatter.

May the shinning of this picture never die. And may the talents who would shine or would have shone brighter, or much brighter than these ones come to limelight, and remain ablaze, in the name of their Creator and Maker, who does give all good things, amen.

PARALLEL PEOPLE

Parallel people don't meet
Each, to his own sheet
Every man on their own feet.

Four people in a room
One with the broom
Sweeping away bloom to boom.

Many people facing doom
Then four people decided to tweet,
While the other folks enjoy their fleet.

To the bird that tweets
God please give him wings,
To those Jaga who ban
God confuse their anthem and antenna.

Parallel people in chopper with wings
Parallelogram people in kilogram deals.

Being young is a blessing
Ageing too, is a blessing
The young shall grow
While the aged take their rest in peace.

May the young not kill the aged
And may heaven not allow the aged to kill the young.

Hence, may I never see my ears, except in the mirror.
Lord, may affliction never rise the second time!

EIGHT DAYS TO ELECTION NIGERIA TO DECIDE

Eight days to election, Nigeria to decide
A Articulating
B Bolatinunu
P Peter Obiii

A B P, People's All Labouring, Not in vain!

Eight days to election, Nigeria will decide
Whether to privatize
Make a damn payment for the roasted corn,
Or go and verify beyond doubts!

A Articulating
B Bolatinunu
P Peter Obiii

The people deceiving people
The progressives that are retrogressive
Or those labouring for dignity, for no man shall labour in vain!

Eight days to election Nigeria must decide
Whether to be strangers
Whether to be touts
Or to be traders
Seven, six, five, four, three, two and just one moment it's real.

Eight days to election Nigeria shall overcome
Cash, cashless shackles
Charge, charges bundles

Hate, confusion, illusion, delusion, defusion
Just few more days, this land we hope shall be great again, if we cast our votes rightly.

Eight days to election Nigeria makes me fear
See how we running, hell helter skelter
Right, left, round and around
Suffering and smiling, killing one another
While they lay and laugh, lying to everyone like they're born to lie.

Eight days to election Nigeria rolls and rides
Ticking tick tick tock, tock tock and tock
Time ever rolling, rolling fast, fast faster
We pray thee oh time heal us!

FREEDOM IS COMING TOMORROW

I hear the chains of slavery drop
Wearing bands of bravery atop
Freedom is coming tomorrow!

I hear the shackles of pain flee
Tearing down chuckles of hours wee,
Yes I hear, freedom is coming tomorrow!

Bonds of penury unfolding,
Dismantling, disentangling, disengaging
Freedom is coming tomorrow, look yonder!

Ropes of hate in rates so high
Scopes of fate in gates so nigh
Freedom in labour! Laboureth not in vain!

Stocks of vine in deep gutters
Flocks divine asleep in batters
Lucks locked up in blocks like cocks and docks
Hmm, hmm, freedom laboureth!

Bondages of shame for fame
Rampages on name by game
Homages the same, the blame still lame
This freedom must come!

Bloodsuckers in robes as leaders
Killers in crowns as mediators
Demons in uniforms as monitors
Freedom must come tomorrow!

Sweats and labour and prayers
Feats defeat us helplessly
Heat hit us in broadway, waylaying
In broad daylight they lick and launder blood
This freedom will not labour in vain!

Green vegetations starving of water
Fertile lands drying of seeds
Fields fading away fruitlessly
Freedom must come tomorrow!

Teeming brains firing cracks
Youthful blood cracking brains
Drugs, cartels, brothels, rituals
Lively populace dwindling in hunger
Lovely space swindling in anger;
Freedom must come tomorrow!

Home and abroad, we prepare for change
Far and wide, we plan for next level
Up and down, we hope anew
Yet, vultures tear us apart,
Freedom! Freedom!! Freedom!!! Answer to your name!

Fears surround all the ballots
And tears around all the harlots,
Gears, to stampede all the patriots
But bears will concede to the chariots
Because ours is the time for freedom!

The future is now, never ask how
The jackals, the hyenas, the strangest wild

It's time for the cow to bow in the row they sow.

Lift up your heads, ye gates of brass
These gates so ancient, barbaric and ungodly
Lift up your bars, ye gates of crossbars
These bars that bar stars and mar superstars
Hear it loud and clear, Freedom is coming!

Arise and shine, for thy light has come
Mama, prepare for freedom, it will be great
Freedom is coming tomorrow.

God bless Nigeria,
God bless Africa!

BUFFALO SOLDIER

These eyes have seen hell
More than the blood from my cell,
These shoulders have bore burdens
More than stains and pains,
These breasts have been troubled
Bitter heart, mind, soul, and spirit battered!

These plasters cannot mar me
Because my pain is bigger than this flesh
I am a buffalo soldier, fighting for a green land
This blood is my witness.

They can only be thugs
Together with their bedbugs,
They can only remain slaves
Held back tight in their caves,
But this blood is my witness
You dare, not me, suppress.

Someday, we will clean the mess
And we will no longer have it less.

Buffalo soldier, I am
Oh hear me sing redemption song
Because freedom is coming tomorrow!

ON THE BORDERLINE

I hear loud laughter on the top of the roof
Even when the house is ablaze without a fireproof,
Instead they merry wearing only a waterproof.

They can't see the gate has been locked
And the exit hardened and blocked
Yet they celebrate, celebrating prejudice.

They think it's a game of peace
But it's piece will piss on the price
Because nature will always parcel justice.

I hear them jubilate, but there's actually mourning
Mourn, mourn this morning, I say mourn
For only in the morning can you have strength to mourn.

On the borderline, I see padlock
Change got stuck
Exchange rate in a town hall
Ready for cornmeal from a con company.

The wings of those whose flight were cut short
The steps of those whose journey were aborted
The smiles of those whose happiness were buried,
I see those ones who plot and plan, cheering their cherries
Cherishing their crime and concoction,
Professing, processing, and pronouncing evil.

This borderline has been bordered
Have you ever thought of how to unlock it

Who would teach you escape means and escape routes?
Wait, bigotry is worse than purgatory.

Ethnic profiling just like in the titanic
Chronic sabotaging like satanic
Renewing dashed hope for a crashed microscope,
Watch well, this borderline you crossed!

Antagonizing the future, jeopardizing the leopard
This gekco you fed to the lizard
This chameleon you fed to the crocodile
This dolphin you fed to the whale
This cobra you fed to the python
This boar you fed to the anaconda
Remember anything can be hungry and nothing is beyond feeding upon!

Beware of those who cheer you, especially when you are on the chair
For the heart of a man is desperately wicked.

The blue hall, the town army, the wild coats
Sailing on the pain of the people's boats
Prevailing on the drowning goats,
This borderline is a wall, beware!

In black, moody, brooding
Feeling the neighborhood,
Childhood is gone, and adulthood stolen
Bothering on the borders, with those onboard
Yet the people boarding never bothered!

This burden on the borderline is a frontline

It will quake the waterway, the highway and the airway
Check this lock, and pray for the luck to open heavens.

ABRACADABRA (ii)

Strange voices yelling from all corners of the world. They are crying in pain, like there is a mourning in the land. Like a woman in labour, travailing to bring forth life.

Fathers sigh, they hiss uncontrollably. Because their own lives no longer make sense to them. How sure are they of their children's?

The trees stand still, there is no air anywhere to help them breathe. Their roots wail, wailing for water, because the waters have dried.

Animals have rejected their jungle and habitats. They roam on the streets, devouring humans.

They pride in the courts, not lawns. Because they have bought the umpires, and crippled the players.

This journey is a millennial one, like a century for centuries to come. But the centenary will be celebrated too.

Aliens have taken the earth, the earth is no more humanitarian. They have chased humans to hell, and planted their hermophrodites.

Monsters whip angels, and tell them there's no heaven. And God is silent. Hence his silence convinces them of his inexistence.

The road to the palace is naturally like the kingdom, it needs not be like a cemetery.

They have done their schemes with their allies together, and challenged the gods. Who dares them!

Of the impunity and audacity, that ravage authenticity, that's one atrocity power has created.

Shades of alloys that murder, and sheds of convoys that plunder, sharp shovels that dig graves and short spades that bury nations. See them, clowns dancing with stolen crowns.

Stampeding dreams and puncturing skulls, careless of life, yet wanting to lead life. Miniatures of satan, in traditional attires and religious apparels. Mean men of occultic order, ascending and descending.

The status quo is not afraid of a new narrative, and the doctored patient is not scared of the hospital because his brother is the nurse.

Elders whose footsteps should lead the young to paradise, statesmen whose footmarks should clear the doubts for the youths, ambassadors whose footprints should give clues to the unborn, see them here, closing up every trace in all nooks and crannies.

Fatigue, tiredness, trauma and dilemma, all catching up with them whereas even karma hasn't arisen.
Divide and rule, now or never, no one but me.

Gray hairs come with wisdom, but it's unfortunate and factual that the mad and the fool grow both old and gray.

Eagles fear to soar, but vultures enjoy flights. Lions fear to roar, but peacocks pride in shame. A land so desolate in deeds and actions.

They will choke you, and pretend it is choking. They will grill you, and pay the bill
They will nail you, and send you the mail
They will jail you, and shout bail is free.

A land of moral decadence, unperturbed about injustice and perverts.
Boldly and comfortably going down the abyss.

ELUU PEE!

Four people tweeting in a room
Striving to wipe away the gloom
Turning things around without structure,
Eluu Pee 76!

Four people tweeting in a room
Only to have a big boom
Challenging every status quo,
Eluu Pee 77!

Four people tweeting in a room
Captivating the whole classroom
Teaching professors numbers
And fixing the cisterns like plumbers,
Eluu Pee 78!
Obii! 79!

Four people tweeting in a room
They have gone viral
And their ideology, spiral
Home and in diaspora
Fighting to kill a national cobra;
Godfatherism, cabalism, bribery and corruption
Eluu Pee! 80 Obii 81!
Eluu Pee! 82 Kererenke 83

Keypad warriors, wailers and lamentators
They say we labour in vain as commentators
Despite the state of the nation
Despite the fate of the caution
They sheepishly gather their tribesmen

And foolishly scatter another kinsmen,
Obii! 84 Kererenke 85
Obi Nwannem 86!

Four people tweeting in a room
Giving the world a sleepless night
Changing the narratives, staging a fight
Intellect, wisdom, knowledge, ability, might
Eluu Pee 87! Obii 88!

The yark will lose in the yatch
His manhood will not be in the mood
And the professor will not profess or prophesy
Surely, they will hear shouts of joy
Eluu Pee 89! Eluu Pee 90!
Obi! 91! Obii 92!

Then the coconut heads, the wrong generation
Those four people tweeting in a room
They will tweet the noise on social media
And Eluu Pee to infinity!

THE COCONUT HEAD HAS CHANGED THE NARRATIVE

They have suddenly forgotten to roast corn by the wayside, and help the poor woman carry her baby... because the youths are no longer smiling.

They have stopped carrying sachet water in tray, on their head, pretending to be selling same on the road, on traffic, thanks to the reasonable Nigerian youths.

They no longer roast bóle (plantain) along the road, while their heavily armed security, crew, press, and convoy act and stay alert..." because suffer don taya us."

Their first ladies no longer pretend to be frying akara (beans ball) by the side of the road for a few minutes, while the mass media go agog with their magical talents...all because the youths have woken up.

The other has resorted to hairdressing, footballing, ice-creaming, churching, fake one on one interactions, yet hasn't told us who gave the order, because of recent gathering, resulting to fear and trembling. The desperation is second to none.

They were mocking the labourers, forgetting that there's dignity in labour, and every labourer deserves his wages.... because the Nigeria youths have changed the game.

These politicians don't talk about giving us water, providing electricity, building schools, creating jobs, constructing roads, building hospitals, and other basic social amenities, because they have become ashamed of making the same promises since Nigeria got independence... besides, we have realized they have fooled us for ages, and the only ones we have, had been the ones built by the colonial masters.

They gather and choose puppets for themselves, or bulldogs against the people...yet, they swore oaths to work for the people.

They have stopped eating meals with pupils, and the trader-money has disappeared, because there is no money even in the central bank. Funny people, playing with timebomb.

The ones who take convoys to register their toddlers in school and make a show of it, have refused to show us if those children have done their doctoral programs... because the youths are tired of even their certificates.

They no longer step into mud and flood to show the youths that they are humans indeed, because that format "don cast las las."

Those who sweep have gotten tired, their waists have broken, their brooms have aged, the floor is clean, and nowhere to sweep again, hence they are renewing their hope.. but the Nigerian masses are not smiling.

They are now attending parties, invited or uninvited, organized or unorganized, they are shaking hands, cracking jokes, greeting everyone, seeming humble but actually humbled by the youths, because it is no more business as usual.

Youths, the very youths, teeming and brilliant, wasting and idling away, while their own children school and work in their choice part of the world....now, they have suddenly remembered the youths...

the leaders of tomorrow, the tomorrow they have vowed never to come!

The youths they forced to become robbers, pickpockets, prostitutes, touts, agberos, cultists, dropouts, homeless and hopeless, ..the youths the government, the society and powers that be ruined and buried...they are now seeking the face of the Nigerian youths! Lazy Nigerian youths.

See the plank and wood, one used to cross a certain gutter. Bold to mount his picture, he constructed a bridge of the children, by the children and for the children, after eight years of assembling and representing.

The other one hired heavy-duty machines and divided roads into two, because of an opponent.... this one is a leader, leading humans, to wherever he so desires... the things that happen only in Nigeria. He is still seating, sitting and relaxed.

They have stopped making promises, because their fools have woken up. They are now bent on more rigging, more violence, unfortunately, they are dealing with the wrong generation, coconut head, digital wizards.

They mess up everything, everywhere, every system,....when a digital generation is at alert, all out, watching with keen interest, and equally ready for a positive change, because we cannot continue like this. No way!

Hunger has finished us, markets are burning, monies don't exist. These people have finished this land! Even hell isn't like this!

Broad day robbery, lying with a straight face, even while on camera replay. Poor God, what have these people not done and what haven't we seen?

It's no longer the time for them to move in long convoys, waving and expecting a total lockdown and shutdown, ... people now challenge their convoys...they have debased themselves to that, and I see more, a very unthinkable one coming.

The youths are questioning everything; curious and inquisitive... this country will turn around. Hopefully, for good.

Look at them, mean and hardhearted, unconcerned and ungodly...these men have forgotten the names and traces of some nations where they packed monies to...yet they are packing and looting. And people are starving, thirsting, like in wartimes.

They are no more roasting bóle, frying akara, roasting corn, selling sachet water, along the roadside, because of election... the coconut head, the wrong generation has changed the narrative.

Time shall come, when they would be nameless, faceless, because I know they are already shameless.

It's retirement time, turn by turn, we are retiring these chameleons and scorpions, changing into any suitable colour to sting the masses. Nature, will not spare them. Retribution, will not. Heaven and earth will not either!

DEAR CHARLES SOLUDO

The finest of gold, and green refined diamond. Dazzling brain and teeming heart of a matured brewery. Lovely and lively team in one legend.. greetings, I bring you.

Nobody can take it away what you stood for; excellence, what you stand for; intelligence, and what you would stand for; competence. Sure, we know, no matter what flies down like a bird to attack the nest.

We can't forget that melodious tenor, of brass that punctures the grass, and shatters the glass ceiling...yes, it is still echoing and re-echoing in our ears, like reverberations and ripples.

Dear Charles, he was once a saint. But only sinners can be saint, after all.

It's not a crime to profess, but it depends on the process and progress of the professor and profession, whether or not he can be a professional through professionalism.

I have watched with fear how suddenly, the grand is aligning and allying to rebrand the brand, a brand that once bordered on competence, soundness, credibility, authenticity, dignity, integrity, honesty, humility, accountability, transparency and virtues... unfortunately in the malicious and suspicious ways... return, return.

Disappointed? Yes! Hopeful? Oh Yes!

It's still early, there's yet a chance left. Pick it up and make unbelievable amends. It's too early and so disheartening, that a soldier could fear the battlefield. Remember, wars are not fought at home. And wars won at home have marred unity, family and posterity.

I am not yet cold-hearted, I am still optimistic, that my Charles, our Soludo would deliver. Remember, all eyes are on you, no escape route... besides we are rooting for you. You have to deliver. It's a must!

I have taken certain utterances as slip of tongue, I have taken some actions as mistakes, I have also seen some moves as contests, I have tagged some competitions as set-ups, I have termed some motives as passionate communion ... nice, I don't hold them against you. There's a room, you can perform wonders, I trust you. Surely, you will have to perform miracles. No option!

The events unfolded so soon, in confusing quick successions, setting a terrible notions in motion, having them appear like friction, but I still have this craving that our very own Soludo would crack the big nuts...yes, he will. Soludo, you will definitely!

Whatever the grand progressives could not labour, then who else could? It is a beautiful labour that makes a grand progressive. It is a unique labour that brings a progression of dignity. Hence, your labour shall never be in vain. On this ground, the grand will be earthquaking.

You are our central bank, yes, we bank on you. Therefore, you will bank on us. You shall mint, mint us. A world bank, you are. Not just Ala Igbo.

Make hay while the sun shines, because what goes around comes around.

Soludo, please follow peace with all men because Chukwu Ma. Always remember that.

I can't just give up on you like that, because I have eyes, eyes that are neither normal nor ordinary. Don't shake nor break your ladders, for these rungs are so high and lofty, falling off them would be more dangerous than tsunami.

Please Dear Soludo, Anambra is blessed. Anambra is blessed having you. Allow those blessings to flow through you, in you, on you, for you, from you, and of you.

Remember, Dim Odimegwu Ojukwu's last wish, Peter. His last wish? Peter! On that bill board? Peter!

I tell you, everyone would shine, no matter who outshines, destiny has no query to answer.

Until I hear from you, this is my first letter to you, dear Charles.

I believe in you, I shall not tremble, I shall not be disappointed, I shall not be fooled, I shall not be mocked, I shall not regret, I shall not be doubtful, I shall not be hopeless, I shall not be helpless, if and only if you will allow God to use you.

Many people will not tell you this. But I can't forget how you melted our hearts and exhibited absolute brilliance. Bravery isn't only in the face of danger.
Charity begins at home.
Home is God.
A kingdom divided against itself cannot stand.

Ulo Wú Chi.
Onuru ube Nwanne agba la oso.
Igbo bu otu.
Igwe bu Ike.

I have so much to write, but a word is enough for the wise, more especially to a dear professor.

Thank you Prof.,
Ngozi Olivia Osuoha.

MY TWO BILLION DOLLARS

Up north I climb
To search for oil,
But down south, I drill
To flare gas
And kill with soot.

Thousands of feet
Rocks I meet,
Thousands I quarry
Water, I marry.

Poppy yes, poppy yes
My bank is large
The vault breaks,
My two billion dollars.

Hunger on their face
Denial in their place
Torments for their space.

Bills on medical trips
Oil to grease the rig
Rigging for oil
Oiling the rigging
The rigged rigger
And the rigger, rigged
All with my two billion dollars.

Wells, blocks, wells of oil blocks
Up north, watering the rig
Down south, rigging the water

Oil boom, water boom
Desert, wilderness, stones and rocks,
My two billion dollars.

Game, play, chess, draft
Leader, leading, leadership
Anointing oil, oiling water
Holy water, watering oil
Oh my two billion dollars.

Rags for camouflage, pebbles for armoury
Skulls for agreements, lives for diplomacy
Families for vengeance, vanquishing
Generations in turmoils, decades of bondage,
Sealed with my two billion dollars.

Roasted academics, burnt survival
Buried hope, damaged future
Ancestors living, unborn dying
My two billion dollars, drowning.

The oil of unity
The water of diversity
Watered oil of peace
Oily water of blood,
Scam, desperation, deceit
Sweeping my two billion dollars.

Civilization is life
Ignorance is death
Betrayal is retrogression
Lies are graves
Stunts are gravitational pull

Analogue is outdated
Digital is updated,
My two billion dollars mourn.

Two hundred million
Two billion dollars
Humans and currency
Stooling, purging, coughing
No evil deed shall go unpunished.

Hospitals without health
Schools without knowledge
Places without road
Humans without life
Heads without body
Eyes without sight
Mouths without words
But my two billion dollars can help.

Lazy youths for next level
Old rulers fantastically corrupt
A people overtaken,
Poor land dwelling on curse
Oh my two billion dollars.

Caged, bound, limited
Terrorized, brutalized, antagonized
Agonized, demonized, mesmerized
My two billion dollars, weep.

Feet, feet, upon feet
Deep, deep, upon depth
Debt, debt, across the globe

Death, death, death, upon death
Infested, incited, instigated,
My two billion dollars, roar.

Oil up there, lock down
Oil down here, crack down
Water up there, one, one, one
Oil down here, one, one, one,
My two billion dollars, beckon.

Black land, bitter land
Dark people, bitter souls
Troubled, angered, embattled
Battered, butchered, polluted
My two billion dollars, wail.

Wasted effort, intentional waste
Duped, cajoled, mocked
Cover-up, undercover,
My two billion dollars, buried underneath.

The rebel, the revolutionist, the freedom fighter
The activist, the protagonist, the unionist
The movements, the revolutions
The rebellion, the freedom, the emancipation
Someday, my two billion dollars will pay the bills.

TWILIGHT OF HONOUR

There's no more health in health workers, they have ruined the health sector.

Scholars now score own goals, because they are frustrated and intoxicated.

The army is now a band of ruthless men, they have abandoned armour, honour and taken up offensive and atrocious odour.

Those that minister now administer terror, horror and liquor. They spew and spit poison, endangering the populace.

Lawbreakers rebrand as lawmakers, and murderers regroup as caregivers. They bandage life only to set it ablaze.

The ones who execute, only deal with prisoners.

And those Judicious ones justify Judas. They blame and fine Jesus for ever coming to the world.

Twilight of honour. There is nothing, no one honourable. Honour is so detached from them.

They steal on cameras, and kill on surveillance. They rape on televisions, and kidnap on tournaments. Honour is dwindling, what a twilight!

They are aliens, allegedly humans. But humans in demon's skin. Not a word from them is near truth or true.

Call them honourable at your own expense. Judge them accurate at your own detriment. They divide and rule, and call it divine.

Have you seen rivers of blood? I mean flooded ocean, where flesh and blood is water.

Scholars take oaths and make covenants, they compromise to the least, provided they are included in the list.

Bigots have infested the land like maggots, they bite like insects and commit incest. They inject infection to the weak, strong and able. The twilight of honour is here!

People in the education sector have lost their senses. They have nothing to write home about.

Industries have folded and left, packed up, they have taken to their heels because this land is choking and suffocating.
However, they thrive somewhere else.

They will never improve on electricity because they import power generators.
They have sworn never to build refineries, because they have tank farms in-broad and out-broad.
If you dare raise a voice for such, you become non-existent.

They feast on humans, talents, dreams and visions to stay afloat their own interests.

The information arena has been a cinema, just for entertainment, unfortunately grievous comedy.

The orientation agency is an extension of their gameplay and game plan. Nothing progressive actually emanates from it.

Agriculture is as dead as the ancestors. Porous, poor, plastic, poisonous, and without any password or passmark. The honour in twilight.

Filthy leaders, inhumane rulers, heartless beasts, they paddle only the titanic... Destruction and destructive, deceiving us to believe otherwise.

They can neither captain themselves nor pilot others, hellbent on catastrophe.

Scholars happily score own goals, and celebrate same like legends.

The health sector has no health; very unhealthy.
Recreation and tourism have evaporated like thin gas, there is no hope for tomorrow. That's an honour in twilight... fading away... furiously, fastly!

Elders use their unborn for supper, and their successors as collaterals. They buried every chance of them dying. They appear to be immortal. Where do we go from here?

Reprobate minds, they all. Reproducing maps, dead footprints and lifeless thumbprints...no trace of future. Honourless routines. Sad!

Congresses of shameless congressmen and mannerless congresswomen, witches and wizards of the lowest order, flying day and night to distablize a people.

They have numerous wealths in nations of the world, they loot as though they are gods and deities, like spirits beyond destruction. What manner of men!

Dead conscience, otherwise, how shouldn't a conscience bring home fortune from abroad? Roads, schools, orderliness, sanity, production, hospitality, what a twilight indeed!

They are great in branding the youths whatever names, but they are the core cause of whatever happening to the youths. Talented youths wasted, wasting and yet to waste, who knows?

Outfits: formal and informal, that focus against the people, against the masses....anti-people.

Twilight of honour. Honour in twilight.
A fate so twisted in a twist of fate.
A twist in fate that fate itself is fatefully twisted trying to untwist itself from fate.

Many a time, an honour in twilight or a twilight in honour and or of that of honour is not or may not be fate but rather ill-fated by the government.

DEAR KINGSLEY MOGHALU (PART ONE)

Dear Kingsley,
If you don't see youths on election day
It's because they have dreams
So they are afraid of dying.

If you don't see youths on election day
It's because they are afraid their votes won't count.

If you don't see youths on election day
It's because the old politicians have refused to let go of power.

If you don't see youths on election day
It's because politics is about rigging.

If you don't see youths on election day
It's because they have lost confidence in politicians.

If you don't see youths on election day
It's because politicians never fulfill any campaign promises.

If you don't see youths on election day
It's because it's never free and fair, neither free nor safe.

If you don't see youths on election day
It's because their blood may go down the drain like the blood of baboons.

If you don't see youths on election day
It's because politicians incite violence and heat up the polity.

If you don't see youths on election day

It's because election is a do or die affair.

If you don't see youths on election day
It's because youths are not empowered.

If you don't see youths on election day
It's because politicians use them as thugs and ballot box snatchers.

If you don't see youths on election day
It's because bullets have been bought to blow off their heads at polling stations.

If you don't see youths on election day
It's because nothing is working.

If you don't see youths on election day
It's because they always postpone elections at dying minutes.

If you don't see youths on election day
It's because their leaders sell them for votes.

If you don't see youths on election day
It's because they are tired of voting.

If you don't see youths on election day
It's because the civil and civic right are sour on their tongue.

If you don't see youths on election day
It's because they have been disenfranchised.

If you don't see youths on election day
It's because politicians steal their mandates.

If you don't see youths on election day
It's because none of the politicians' children are in Nigeria.

If you don't see youths on election day
It's because they have spent all their energy shouting, and making some noise, all on deaf ears and mean hearts.

HAPPY BIRTHDAY TO THE VILLAGE GIRL

Sound the gong so loud in the hills
Let the alarm ring noisily and steadily across the waters
Blow the trumpet down all the valleys, far and near
Let heaven and earth rejoice
For here comes a tiny voice in the wilderness!

Happy birthday to this village girl
That African girl, black and bold
Costlier than gold, she's to behold!

Happy birthday to me, onward a hollow furrow
Following a fallow marrow, in a land of pain for gain
Yes, born, we were borne
Victors and victims, alike warriors and soldiers
Dancers and chanters, upon performers and reformers
We were borne, yes born in a land of sorrow for morrow.

Happy birthday to the village girl, the village girl of Africa
Crude, timid, poor, hungry and vulnerable
Choking in a soil of toil and turmoil
Boiling, foiling, fuming, freezing, fainting and failing
Yes, exactly, I was born there, here.

Like flags, we will keep flying
As for trophies, we will keep winning
At our feet, we will them, keep laying
Lonely and dreary, alone or teamwork, this field surely shall bear fruits, sweet fruits of memorable story.

Happy birthday to me, the Julyite.
Happy birthday to the village girl.

I am Ngozi Olivia Osuoha, the African girl, that African girl, the village girl!

THE TOWN CRIER

A townhall different from red and blue, posing for the marathon ahead, definitely not a relay.

There's famine in the land, winding up, trying to settle on a troubled sea, maybe actually for a replay.

This logarithm has crossed the arithmetic and has refused to progress geometrically, unfortunately without a foreplay. Hence Pythagoras is confused to prove any theorem.

Forebears of folklores have forfeited fortunes amidst misfortunes, and cocktails.

A townhall different from blue, black and blue, reddened in the presence of fiery furnace, so hardened, pretending to be furniture and overtures.

The towncrier is weak, his throat is patched, his knees are feeble, his elbows are shaky and shackles have overtaken his voices.

Burnt beans for fifty million fresh troops, trooping out along in parts through paths unknown, unlocked and unnecessary.

She is here to goof around, her own worries war her like a battalion yet she is a stallion.

Cry me a river, these riverbanks are bursting. Nothing is shielding even a drop, believe me, these dead folks behave like they have hypnotized God.

Cry me a river!

But nearer and nearer draws the time, the time that shall surely be, when the earth shall be filled with the glory of God as the waters cover the sea....yes, that hymnist was very right.

THE STATE AND ITS GATE

Even history fluctuates and gets truncated sometimes. Especially when narrators, actors and players want to have their way.

Permutations, combinations, probabilities, theorems, hypotheses and the likes don't work in Nigeria, so your little brain would fail you amidst the circle of postulations.

Critical thinkers and think-tanks go mad if they overstretch their limits. Your tiny brain would fail you willingly, consciously, stupidly, insanely, poorly and regrettably.

Facts are fictions too.
Logics are irrationalities too.

If you think errors are errors, you are right,
If you think errors are not errors, you are still right.

Opinions, are burdens borne and bore inwardly.
They could also be burdens bore outwardly especially when they boomerang.

You go into the laboratory for experiments, practicals, innovations, inventions, discoveries and developments, you don't do all or any of that outside the laboratory.

Realities aren't fantasies, illusions aren't truths, fallacies aren't formulas, only compound fools act behind the scene, legends take the stage.

Complex, reflex, apex, they all flex.

What am I saying? Far from what you are thinking! But I mean in Nigeria, for Nigeria, with Nigeria, under Nigeria, around Nigeria, your minute head can't crack any coconut.

Go on anyway, formulate, postulate, insulate, encapsulate, calculate, coordinate, cooperate, inaugurate, rate late or date fate, your tiny brain can't accommodate the gate and its state, nor the state and its gate, because hate is the state of the gate.

SHAME TO GOD

Is there anyone in Nigeria who doesn't have a bank account, even one, two, three, four and more accounts? But I tell you it is easier to find them than find anyone who doesn't belong to a church. Even atheists, some of them were once Christians or belonged to a religious group. Moslems have their own religion. Converting a moslem or an atheist, traditionalist, to Christianity or another religion is a different thing all together.

I find it difficult to comprehend that pastors were sacked because they couldn't grow a church, except you tell me that you are running a business, then I can understand you.

Some people are defending it daily with all their energy, it is well. Nigeria and Nigerians remain thickly unfathomable to me. This land makes me more confused how I landed here. In fact I always question God humanly.

This sack reminds me of my little experience with intercontinental bank, as a marketer. Daily meetings, reports, prospects, trekking, looking for customers and money. It was not funny.

We could even manage customers, but the trauma you face with your senior colleagues during meetings, reports...horrible questions and intimidations, are enough to frustrate your dream and damage your self-esteem.

Then Access bank happened, my group nationwide was laid off.

After some months I went back to another bank which I had earlier rejected. This time around, less pay and more trauma. The regional meeting of my group was weekly, there, they abuse even your parents, relatives, friends, asking why your cabal/balance hasn't grown. It didn't take me time to leave. In short, let me stop here for now.

Since this sack saga, my banking experience has been playing and replaying in my head, and I see no difference with what has happened. I don't attend your church though, I could be wrong. But then, Nigeria, We Hail Thee!

For religion, I know one thing and that I believe so strongly, if there's anything you have proudly done to God, in the name of service, it is nothing but bringing SHAME TO GOD!

LADIES, MODEL YOURSELVES!

This lady that just got married/wedded, I hope you would just go home and enjoy your marriage. Pray and live each day under God's care, because if troubles and problems are 100 in the world, being a Nigerian makes them 200. I hope you don't.....

This is the first time I am seeing your picture, although I have heard your name a few times. Events recently have dug up your beliefs, stands, words...

The other one that sells digital spirits or something makes more sense to me oo, although I got to actually know her and what she does lately.

The worst part is that no matter how off and odd we are, we must have followers, the madder you are, the more teeming your followers.

What is actually wrong with WOMEN, especially today's ladies?

We have so become empty and baseless that anybody could be our role model.

BURNT ORANGE

I was a bit chocolate and beautiful, my hair was long too, I was neither burnt nor orange. How come!

I am confused to ask, and more confused to answer. Nobody seems to want to ask or answer. And none has the answer at hand.

Have we been sacrificed as a burnt offering?
To which God, our own God, their own gods or deities?

The land is quaking, and their hand is baking
The waters are roaring, and their gutters are soaring
Humans have become refuse, and homes have turned refuse-dumps.

Beautiful orange is now disgusting, as sweet as it is, it is now bitter and sour.

Burnt orange, how come!

Even bedbugs are starving. Mosquitoes are protesting. Lice are fighting. Cockroaches are demonstrating, how come!

Two watch each other's back, but here am I, also watching my back, even when I can't see my front. How come?

Brilliant, bright, shouting orange, turning black and dark, like charcoal.

Gas, fuel, oxygen, carbon dioxide, carbon monoxide, all and many more have mixed with hydrochloric acid and sodium chloride...our acidity and alkalinity have frustrated our pH level, our body system is now imbalanced. How just come!

The unity of catapulted fees and the university of somersaulted tuitions would end up crushing more than fifty million youths thereby forcing them to join the army where burnt orange is likely to be waiting for them. Just how come!

The farmer will have no food, the trader will make no money, the funeral homes will have more contracts, and they would deny it ever happened! And nobody gave the order.

The governed governor, governing the governed will appoint those who pick cameras on crime scenes days after, and the orange will be burnt. Just like that.

In less than sixty days, praise singers have turned mourners, lullaby singers have turned lunatics, and nannies have gone home from the rallies. How come, what were they thinking?

Well, the other gang will shock them. The gang of perpetual blind men, the blind bartimaeus... the ones born blind...they have not seen Jesus, but they know Jesus is passing...he will favour them and their family.

I am not here to ronu you, the ronu-ed are already running around, trekking to kilimanjaro to see the kangaroo, it could take them to Limpopo or zambezi. Well, I hope they don't drown in the Nile while making a headway via the Niger, because the congo is suffering some draught and the senegal is temporary not within reach. I see them being served a burnt orange or being used as a burnt offering. Then I will be here, but I won't ask how come?

This my face is not smiling, it is red-hot with smoke because hunger is killing my land. It has become a routine to kill businesses, frustrate dreamers, castrate stallions and blind visioners.

See, this face is not smiling at all. This orange is burnt and still burning. It is burning even right inside my mouth and my head is aching. How come! How long! For how much!

My front is blurry, yet I am watching my back. My back is scary, still I am going forward. How do I get along?

This land that aborts foetuses, how would you regenerate? This land that rebirths ancestors, how do you nurture your youths? This clime that buries offsprings, where are your middlemen and intermediaries?

This orange is burning me, I can't breathe!
Allow the poor to breathe, do not suffocate them!

If flying in the day is bad and not a bat thing, then flying in the night is witchcraft.

Let the poor breathe,
Do not suffocate us.

I AM AFRAID

I am happy that there's someone speaking up about the latest history class we missed or the one our parents never taught us, perhaps.

I fear for this my generation that behaves as if they came from the blues, so alien and uncultured. A generation that has nothing to do with tradition.

Some of our full blown men cannot present kola traditionally because they are neither interested nor ready to learn such cultures. When you discuss such issues with them they tell you how the world has moved on long ago and how archaic you are.

But when we want to marry, bury, celebrate new yam festival or any other culture, we would just either be lost or become so porous that others mesmerize us with cultures and traditions unnecessarily.

In fact, even some titled people don't know the cultures of, or the reasons why they were titled...because money is there.

Jobs, hustles, clubs, societies, businesses, and other things have carried our young men away, I fear for tomorrow.

I don't even want to talk about my fellow ladies, a generation that grabs madness with two hands, a generation of ladies that pray to not have mothers-in-law, and I wonder who bewitched them. A set that so much focuses on fashion and material things, one that their breasts, bums, toes, nails, eyes, ...are so manmade and unreasonably spilling over, that the flashier the best.

I am so afraid of my generation, the ones to come make it more cumbersome and worrisome. Fakery has given birth to lust, materialism, ungodliness, quest and aggressive adventures for money, fame, marriage....

Aren't you surprised how ladies look inside the church, and how men too?

So baseless, unconcerned, empty, floating, readily available for any trend, be it demonic or lunatic.

This Mgbeke/village girl is tired, but Maazi please keep doing your best, at least there's still a remnant after all, God himself promised to restore us if He sees a remnant.

But to the parents, those our old school parents who have done their beautiful best to instill treasures in us, wherever you are, may heaven and earth bless you, your heart, body and soul, amen. If you finally leave the stage for us and to us, I fear, I am afraid.
May God guide us, amen.

ALL EYES ON THE JUDICIARY

This coconut head has gone pass a juvenile, but hasn't been to Juventus.

Living on planet earth has taught her many things, but she hasn't been to Jupiter.

Nonetheless she knows there is nothing money cannot do, because money answereth all things… no wonder Judas kissed his master for thirty pieces of silver, yet the same choked his throat.

All eyes on the judiciary, whether they execute injustice or legislate bribery.

When Peter angrily cut of someone's ear, Jesus quickly healed the man, still when poor Jesus, was brought before Pontius Pilate, abracadabra people preferred thieves to him.

No wonder, Peter this time around is calling for calm. All eyes on the judiciary.

King herod beheaded John the baptist because of his mistress, nobody queried him. All eyes on the judiciary.

We will neither sink nor drown in Jordan, Moses is leading the levites and levite is a Moses. He has the Ten Commandments….he's in the judiciary.

Joseph's brothers sold him, and he later landed in prison via false accusation and allegation. But Portiphar's wife couldn't seduce Pharoah when he rose to bless Joseph.

The Judith sharing the envelopes and the Jonah avoiding Nineveh don't know that there's a fish to vomit the tax and there's a free transporting shark to Nineveh. All eyes on the judiciary.

When the time is right, ask Joel, your daughters shall prophesy, your sons shall see visions and your elders shall dream dreams. And your tearful years shall be restored.

On the feast day, on the seventh feast day, like warriors and dancers, like soldiers and strong men, you shall sing and blow your trumpets round Jerusalem, I say round Jerusalem, and the walls of Jericho shall come crumbling, perpetual crumbles because there are eyes on the judiciary.

Then, you will hear the Cherub, you will also hear the Seraph. You will see them in green and white robes...green and white gold.

All eyes on the judiciary, perversion of justice has reached the high heavens.
See it crumbling down like the tower of babel.

57 HEARTY BONGO NOISE

I can hear the disco gunshots all the way from Congo, as I chase the wall gecko through Limpopo, but the noise is deafening.

Play me bongo, If you want me to chase this bingo away because by the time I tame his libido, he would know I am not a dildo.

Make some noise, that deafening noise across the west of Africa is mute. Please play it like a flute, let the piper remember to entertain the pauper, because there is no more ripened pawpaw. They have stolen all of them raw with their claws, jaws and laws.

Over fifty, still counting, power has paralyzed you. It has empowered your greed and made you institute a demonic creed. Hear ye therefore these hearty bongo noise.

Ruining our own Economy
Tearing an entire Community
Ripping our lives Off
Bringing down the West
Trampling on anything African
And baring each of the States
Yet, waving a sleeping ECOWAS!

Hello, make some noise, some hearty bongo noise
Let's dance to the music
It's gonna be ginger and garlic
A total comprehension of the inordinate refraction of a blurry glass prism, reflecting poverty, hunger, death, unemployment, evil and barbarity.

Over a golden bongo noise, a personal music

Family noise, kingdom nuance, power-drunk and intoxicated band of lunatic parade with keyless and pitchless tune of inharmonious melody, a whooping five decades plus!

Isn't that a whole lot of noise?

If a mufti can tear a khaki, or if a khaki tears a mufti, then the bingo can bark uncontrollably.

Bongo is enough noise
Disco is enough party
Congo is a soil of Africa.

BukinaGabMaliNig or BuGaMaNi

Invading an improper fraction is already inverse variation. The probability is off the tangent of the circle. Parallel planets reaching for the abyss... colossal error.

Therefore the almighty formula would have been proper governance, to find the square root of the problem, in order to not raise it to power ^{3} or increase it with the speed of light.

Make noise in your numbers, number your members so that none would be missing. But you would get adequate noise when the palliatives tend to impoverish the lives of the masses. Someone say noise!

57 hearty bongo noise
57 bongo hearty noise
57 noises to heart a hearty bongo.

The bingo is dancing bongo

The bingo is playing disco
And a bongo is playing bongo and dancing disco with his bingo,
He is feeding his libido with a dildo, while playing ludo with a land against the land.

And you think there won't be numerous noise?
Come on make some noise!

Almost a diamond noise,
what a poise so poisonous!

BuGaMaNi in the air*

Oh poor Africa, may these thine gods spare thee.

CHIEF CARGO

Our vessel is about to lopside, and here we are searching for the anchor bolts. We are digging, we have been digging since the seventies to find the certified copies, so that our ship can discharge and take off appropriately.

The chief cargo has some garbage, the opposite of cabbage. So big a luggage, a disgraceful baggage.

Mungo Park is inside the cargo, with a heavy embargo. And the bull of this chief cargo tends to pull us zigzag against gravity and even exposing our nudity.

Chief cargo the bull, please pull out the full degree.

We dream of Chicago but not with tobacco.
We dream of Monaco but not with tornado
We dream of Morocco but not with mosquito.

The judiciary is not portable, therefore not a sizeable majority. However, the masses are neither portable nor sizeable.

Dear Mr Chief Cargo, we are digging, digging for gold but most importantly, to make foundations, strong foundations with pillars, beams and columns, structures that would re-echo virtues, cultures, principles, morals, hopes and aspirations.

This cargo has to take off, more dearly, it will have to anchor, anchor on sure foundations to redeem the past, renew the now and restructure especially the future.

Chief of all cargoes, we planted mangoes, don't give us sour grapes. Don't also give us barren and fruitless fig trees.

Accounting a baboon to build a lagoon, is already a taboo because soon before noon the moon will expose the cocoon.

We are digging, the masses are digging. If the cabinet punctures the cabinet, then the captain may have to sink the cargo. Reason I beckon peace! Please come peace!

Chief cargo, I have heard of the Chicago bull, please take the bull by the horn, and horn before overtaking because this is a long vehicle.

Remember a disorganized choir can end up rendering a war song thereby igniting chaos.

To the Chief Cargo about to lopside, to the vessel anchoring, to the ship sailing, to the captain tossing on the deep blue sea, please bear in mind that this adventurous cargo and voyage of supernatural compass cannot afford to be another titanic. TOMORROW IS JUDGEMENT DAY

The clouds are pregnant, so heavy that the earth is afraid, afraid of the rain. Will the rain fall?

The land is hot, boiling as if it wants to run away. But where can the land run to? Shouldn't it rather wait for a cooling from the rain?

The heavens are rumbling, wobbling and struggling to give birth. What would they birth? Rain! Thunder! Rainbow! Stars! Sun! Moon! Mist! Dew! Fog!
Well, nothing more than the heavenly bodies.

Yes, heaven will not fall.

But what if tomorrow is rapture, because tomorrow is judgement day?

Judgement day? Yes, judgement day. Guess what? Satan is not afraid.

Shall the strong retain the spoil? That, I know not.
But the labourer is still toiling, hoping for a harvest, a bounty harvest.

The matter is weighty and had occupied space, but masses are weightier, earnestly do I hope that they would have their own space to occupy.

Daylight, broad daylight, it was robbed. Crowned, coroneted at midnight. The ungodly hour of the dark. But tomorrow is judgement day.
Will heaven save our land?

Dreams would be live-streamed. It will quake the land, but then can the judiciary disappoint?

Good tidings have been sent, but millions have never heard. Can they hear without a preacher? Lord Almighty, give thy word! Yes, that verdict.

This verdict is all we need to curtail callousness, impunity, audacity, atrocity and calamity. Indeed, it will be a September to remember, either way.

They are fleeing, leaving us to our fate, but what can faith do in the midst of godlessness?

There are things Satan doesn't do, but here, there is nothing we don't do. And that is the height!
Well, tomorrow is judgement day. Would it be rapture as well?
However, surely, it will be a September to remember.

Have the judges sold us?
Have they bought us? Who sold, who bought? How much? What was the price? Mortgage, trade by barter, cash, kind, or slave trade?

How long?

The east, the west, black or white, would it be another colonization?

If a demon can be crazy, then it is not democracy.
If a technology can be crazy, then it is not theocracy.
If the masses can be crazy, then it is far beyond marginalization.

Of what joy is in soured food
Of what sweetness is in bitter fruit
Of what peace is in a troubled land
Of what pride is in lost glory
And of what integrity is in dubious victory?

Well, tomorrow is judgement day and it will be a September to remember.

Hundreds of million people, hundreds of million eyes, looking up to heaven, waiting for tomorrow not to bring sorrow.

Elections are not supposed to be electrocuting.

But here, you have to snatch it, and run with it.

Again, well, tomorrow is judgement day.

Shall it be a verdict of the gods?
A verdict by the gods?
The verdict from the gods?
A verdict against the gods?
Or a verdict above, under, and beyond the gods?

I love my fatherland, I want to know which way Nigeria is heading to.

TIME WILL TELL

Shouldn't there be a waiver, if you want foreigners to leave your country?

Why would they produce their papers if you don't want them to stay? To prosecute/imprison them?

Are there no circumstances, chances and times, when papers and documents don't count, especially in times like these?

Why challenging foreign governments unnecessarily, because they are weak??

Is there something else you are looking for, other than forcing people out of your country, you want them all, dead???

Why not bundle them back home at any cost, and live in your Paradise alone?

Is this diplomacy or Xenophobiacracy?

TIME WILL TELL

DEAR SINGLE LADY

I hope you know that you are not beautiful, and you were created on a forbidden day.

You are good for nothing, and nothing good can come out of you.

You are such a fool, an illiterate and an ingrate.

You grew up wayward, baseless, rascal, promiscuous, ungodly and rude. That's why you are single. And nobody can marry you.

You lack talents, skills, passion, and zeal. You are just a log of wood in the hood, hence you can't attain motherhood.

Dear single lady, there is nothing you can achieve. Achievement has finished, and the God of achievement has forgotten you. You had better killed yourself, you piece of valueless rag.

You can't travel, you can't work, you can't get married, there's nothing you can do. Life has given you the best, which is singleness. Shameless spinster.

Loneliness will kill you, you will not bear a child. The world has left you behind, long ago and ages back.

Husbands are for the well-behaved, well-mannered, godly, decent, clean and brave. You lack all those, so no husband for you.

I hope you know that you have been written off, so bury your head in shame. You are a nobody, and so, you shall remain.

You came from an evil forest, you are possessed, you have a spiritual husband, no in-laws would accept you. No man can put up with you and your dirtiness, you are less than a woman.

Your bad character stinks to the high heavens. Your arrogance irritate the living. Your attitude offend the dead. Heaven and earth, hate you. It is that bad. Sorry.

Dear single lady, I hope you know you are old, very old. Nobody is coming for you. You don't even have a womb. You can neither conceive nor give birth. You have wasted your years. And your youthfulness has been sacrificed to the gods of the land.

See, your male counterparts are doing well. They are flying in the sky. They grew up well tamed and raised by angels. They are all saints and virgins. They are holy to the cherubs and seraphs.

Dear single lady, you have aborted all your babies and slept with all manners of creature. Creation is now fighting against you. You are reaping what you sowed.

When married people are talking, shut up. I say shut up, you know nothing. Therefore, accept and swallow whatever they say or tell you. You are a damn single lady! Empty, wretched and poor fellow. Haggard single termite.

Go for deliverance. Fast for a hundred days, drink no water. Empty your account and sow seeds. After that, go and appease your ancestors. Bathe also for twenty one days in your village river. Gather all your community and confess your witchcraft. Tell them you are the cause of every evil in the land. Except that, you will not get married.

Your mate's children will soon come to ask you out or sleep with you. Remember, you don't have any option. That's what you deserve.

If you don't have bad character, bad life, and bad attitude, why are you still single at this age? Are you not Godforsaken?

Old witch, who will marry you? Proud demon, repent. Your days are numbered!

See, all the good girls have gotten married. They are happily enjoying their matrimonial homes. They are all blessed with beautiful children and lovely husbands.
What have you gained, old single lady?

Hear the pampering and play of the happy homes. Couples, romancing in green light and purple mats, chasing after each other under full blue moon at the beach. Can't you see that they are very happy and blessed? Are you blessed?

You will weep yourself to old age, Methuselah. You have turned a man because you have entered menopause. Your grandmothers didn't enter menopause at your age. At your age, they were still giving birth. Wickedness brought it upon you.

Little things irritate you, because you don't have a husband. You are love-less, angry, single, lonely, frustrated, jobless, homeless, joyless, and bitter. Bitterness has taken over your soul.

Dear single lady, I hope you know that you are not suitable for marriage. The world has left you behind. So go to hell, that's where you belong!

Mmap New African Poets Series

If you have enjoyed *ABRACADABRA*, consider these other fine books in the **Mmap New African Poets** Series from *Mwanaka Media and Publishing*:

I Threw a Star in a Wine Glass by Fethi Sassi
Best New African Poets 2017 Anthology by Tendai R Mwanaka and Daniel Da Purificacao
Logbook Written by a Drifter by Tendai Rinos Mwanaka
Mad Bob Republic: Bloodlines, Bile and a Crying Child by Tendai Rinos Mwanaka
Zimbolicious Poetry Vol 1 by Tendai R Mwanaka and Edward Dzonze
Zimbolicious Poetry Vol 2 by Tendai R Mwanaka and Edward Dzonze
Zimbolicious: An Anthology of Zimbabwean Literature and Arts, Vol 3 by Tendai Mwanaka
Under The Steel Yoke by Jabulani Mzinyathi
Fly in a Beehive by Thato Tshukudu
Bounding for Light by Richard Mbuthia
Sentiments by Jackson Matimba
Best New African Poets 2018 Anthology by Tendai R Mwanaka and Nsah Mala
Words That Matter by Gerry Sikazwe
The Ungendered by Delia Watterson
Ghetto Symphony by Mandla Mavolwane
Sky for a Foreign Bird by Fethi Sassi
A Portrait of Defiance by Tendai Rinos Mwanaka
Zimbolicious: An Anthology of Zimbabwean Literature and Arts, Vol 4 by Tendai Mwanaka and Jabulani Mzinyathi
When Escape Becomes the only Lover by Tendai R Mwanaka
ويَسهَرُ اللَّيلُ عَلَى شَفَتي...وَالغَمَام by Fethi Sassi

A Letter to the President by Mbizo Chirasha
This is not a poem by Richard Inya
Pressed flowers by John Eppel
Righteous Indignation by Jabulani Mzinyathi:
Blooming Cactus by Mikateko Mbambo
Rhythm of Life by Olivia Ngozi Osouha
Travellers Gather Dust and Lust by Gabriel Awuah Mainoo
Chitungwiza Mushamukuru: An Anthology from Zimbabwe's Biggest Ghetto Town by Tendai Rinos Mwanaka
Zimbolicious: An Anthology of Zimbabwean Literature and Arts, Vol 5 by Tendai Mwanaka
Because Sadness is Beautiful? by Tanaka Chidora
Of Fresh Bloom and Smoke by Abigail George
Shades of Black by Edward Dzonze
Best New African Poets 2020 Anthology by Tendai Rinos Mwanaka, Lorna Telma Zita and Balddine Moussa
This Body is an Empty Vessel by Beaton Galafa
Between Places by Tendai Rinos Mwanaka
Best New African Poets 2021 Anthology by Tendai Rinos Mwanaka, Lorna Telma Zita and Balddine Moussa
Zimbolicious: An Anthology of Zimbabwean Literature and Arts, Vol 6 by Tendai Mwanaka and Chenjerai Mhondera
A Matter of Inclusion by Chad Norman
Keeping the Sun Secret by Mariel Awendit
سِجلٌ مَكتُوبٌ لثَائِه by Tendai Rinos Mwanaka
Ghetto Blues by Tendai Rinos Mwanaka
Zimbolicious: An Anthology of Zimbabwean Literature and Arts, Vol 7 by Tendai Rinos Mwanaka and Tanaka Chidora
Best New African Poets 2022 Anthology by Tendai Rinos Mwanaka and Helder Simbad
Dark Lines of History by Sithembele Isaac Xhegwana
a sky is falling by Nica Cornell
Death of a Statue by Samuel Chuma

Along the way by Jabulani Mzinyathi
Strides of Hope by Tawanda Chigavazira
Young Galaxies by Abigail George
Coming of Age by Gift Sakirai
Mother's Kitchen and Other Places by Antreka. M. Tladi
Best New African Poets 2023 Anthology by Tendai Rinos Mwanaka, Helder Simbad and Gerald Mpesse
Zimbolicious Anthology Vol 8 by Tendai Rinos Mwanaka and Mathew T Chikono
Broken Maps by Riak Marial Riak
Formless by Raïs Neza Boneza
Of poets, gods, ghosts. Irritants and storytellers by Tendai Rinos Mwanaka
Ethiopian Aliens by Clersidia Nzorozwa
In The Inferno by Jabulani Mzinyathi
Who Told You To Be God by Mariel Awendit
Nobody Loves Me by Abigail
The Stories of our Stories by Nkwazi Mhango
Nhorido by Siphosami Ndlovu and Tinashe Chikumbo
Best New African Poets 10th Anniversary: Selected English African Poets by Tendai Rinos Mwanaka
Best New African Poets 10th Anniversary: Interviews and Reviews of African Poets by Tendai Rinos Mwanaka
Best New African Poets 10th Anniversary: African Languages and Collaborations by Tendai Rinos Mwanaka
ANTOLOGIA DOS MELHORES "NOVOS" POETAS AFRICANOS 10º Aniversário: Poetas Africanos Da Língua Portuguesa Selecionados by Lorna Telma Zita and Tendai Rinos Mwanaka

www.ingramcontent.com/pod-product-compliance
Lightning Source LLC
Chambersburg PA
CBHW070848160426
43192CB00012B/2357